FIELD OF WANTING

FIELD OF WANTING:
Poems of Desire

Wanda Phipps

BlazeVOX [books]

Buffalo, New York

Field of Wanting: Poems of Desire

Copyright © 2008

Published by BlazeVOX [books]

Printed in the United States of America

Book design by Geoffrey Gatza
Cover photo by Wanda Phipps

First Edition

ISBN 10 : 1-934289-60-4   ISBN 13 : 978-1-934289-60-0
Library of Congress Control Number : 2007938748

BlazeVOX [books]
14 Tremaine Ave
Kenmore, NY 14217

Editor@blazevox.org

publisher of weird little books

BlazeVOX [books]

blazevox.org

2   4   6   8   0   9   7   5   3   1

Acknowledgments

Thanks to the editors and producers of the publications and recordings where some of these poems have previously appeared:

Zither Mood (Faux Press CD-Rom), *Rose Window or Prosettes* (Dusie Press), *Your Last Illusion or Break Up Sonnets* (Situations Press), *Lunch Poems* (BOOG Literature), *After the Mishap* (Faux Press Online Chapbook), *Verses That Hurt: Pleasure & Pain From The Poemfone Poets* (St. Martin's Press), *The Unbearables Anthology* (Autono-media), *O•blek 12: Writing from the New Coast, Valentine Anthology, Agni, How2, Owen Wister Review, The World, Mike and Dale's Younger Poets, Hanging Loose, Big Bridge, Tamarind, Brooklyn Review Online, Pagan Place, National Poetry Magazine of the Lower East Side, Poetic Voices, Red Weather, $lavery: A Cyberzine of the Arts, Blind Date, Long Shot, Handymag, Mentress Moon, Gallery Works, Poemfone Website, Down Under Manhattan Bridge, Transfer, Bombay Gin, Jack, Living With A White Girl, Sensitive Skin, Cocodrillo, a fleshlike rubbery semi-solid mass, City Nights, Reandme.com, About.com, McSweeney's Internet Tendency, A Sheep on the Bus, We,* and *Cover Magazine.*

To my mothers,

those who gave me life, nourishment and inspiration:

E. Marie Phipps, Mary Lou MacMillan and Bernadette Mayer

Contents

Your Last Illusion

A Purist at Heart

                              i am pure madness
if i yell and scream and bleed
              is that pure enough?   is that raw enough?
                    if i wear my sensitivity like a crown
                              is it a tool?
           can i touch you with my frailty?
                    touch you with my vulnerability?
                    is my weakness
                              my strength?

        i heard a woman reading what i'd written to him
              so he'd given it away
                    i'd given it to him and he'd given it away

   someone said a certain scene was too melodramatic
                 when they really meant it was too disturbing
                                             too painful
                                             too real

cuz all they wanted was a little illusion
                 all they wanted was play
                       all they wanted was the same old game

     something about lynching   something about blood
something about getting too close in the night
              and all he really wanted was the same old game

THIS IS HARD---------THIS IS STILL RAW---------THIS IS A FRESH CUT
--------------AN OPEN WOUND--------------------AN OPEN WOMB

  my baby lies over the ocean, my baby lies over the sea
and he said "i have no responsibility for or to you,
                 i have no responsibility for your moods!"

ah yes the woman's moods
     the woman moves from here to there and back again
     and he asks   "what – are you judging me?"

  there wasn't any sound when we made love: very quiet
and he said: "baby" and i said: nothing

"and children this is your paradise"
and i ask myself: am i who i think i am?
and i ask myself: am i the woman scorned?
                          the scorpion about to strike?
                     and uh "vindictive" yeah that's the word
           and am i spiritual, intuitive
                          as well as vengeful and judgmental

am i the woman of your dreams
                    and the villainess of your nightmares
am i the smooth thigh and soft voiced angel

            or am i the cold, distant walking statue
        am i the many pictures in a cubist history
        or abstract lines in a surrealist docu-drama?

sit and listen i say
sit and wait i say
            but it moves   it all moves and the pieces shift
        and i don't know how anymore
            when the longing comes along
                    that loneliness
                        that emptiness hits me
        i don't know how to anymore

                    so i'll yell and scream and bleed
                        and yes get hysterical
            let my madness out----------be my madness
in a safe place--------in an open space----------on a stage----------on a magic
island

                    where everything is sharp as crystal
                        light shining through all the angles

Your Last Illusion
or Break Up Sonnets

(inspired by Ted Berrigan's Sonnets)

1

"what a planet!"
"what a life!"
"what a concept!"
right now I feel
can hardly imagine us not
right now like this
I can sit here for a while
"the muscles around your eyes
how they move in recognition"
can enjoy this for a while
what will my mother say?
who sleeps with who?
I sleep with you
"this is as good as it gets"

2

meet me in Mexico
you silly one come here
and then what then
this is as good as it is odd
"what a concept!"
god's wet dream
my lies aren't long enough
nothing has changed
back to beginning
and now I sleep with books
cry in the bathtub at 3 a.m.
and you remember smiling Wanda
messy mind   shiny sex
in recognition

3

standard ease is a thing worth savoring
the group is busy being a group
in group activity individual loss is secondary
D-train rumbles under apartment
which hovers above
Bistrot La Marseillaise on Flatbush Ave.
a table is a bed is a podium
"what a concept!"
who sleeps with you?
this is less odd than likely
a sure stand in rainy weather
deeper into Brooklyn
down the angry dream
you wait

4

in a mirror–my face still
and also others–faces of others
all still with me
behind eyes–in thought
individual loss does not exist in group activity
"consider this a formal introduction"
turning halfway enough to see your profile
dark blue rings around your pupils
"signs of stress" you say
"what a planet!"
still this is and nothing changed
back to standard ease
cry in the bathtub in recognition
smiling Wanda sleeps with who?

5

your lies aren't long enough
one fuck as good as another
you silly one it goes on
and now I sleep in the bathtub
messy sex   shiny mind
standard ease is a thing worth considering
and now it hovers
a podium is a bed smiling
remember you lying on the grass in Riverside Park
and what a planet you are
seriously don't leave me again
one messy bed lies quietly
above Bistrot La Marseillaise
bright green awning and an open window

6

you say "don't worry" as you fidget
eyes glazed, inward focus
am accustomed now to waking and crying
one messy bed lies
can enjoy this for a while
meet me on E. 7th between C & D
"consider this a formal introduction"
to standard ease and sleepy podiums
bright green weather waits deeper into
shiny mind and dark blue books
still this is a concept worth savoring
what a mess
seriously the group drowns the individual
"I don't believe in the individual" she said

7

consider this turning halfway
back to hovering shiny concepts
right now a mirror still waits
life smiling back at me
away from Flatbush Ave. now beginning
a formal planet of recognition
busy in a blue group
loss of rumbling pupils
surely meeting at the green table again
you'll remember changing nothing
the bright red comforter was a podium
a speaking place for individual lies
active and stubborn you continue running
what's easiest is not always best

8

don't talk about me like a memory
what an easy memory
to lie in
a crazy muscle rules
one fuck as good as an accustomed waking
smile, though not best but brightest other
third place is a cranky rumble seat
speech a knotted stomach
meet me still on the blue wake
savor a vast but formal park
on the edge of a living window
now stress what the mind cannot tell
words a standard drowning
of recognition

9

liberation day comes
April is the month of best sex
smile now feel the energy focused
a planet is an active window
for easiest Sunday ease
drink Irish coffee at 4 a.m.
seeing wasteful lines of worry
in the dark blue mind mirror
breakthrough happens in a green
suddenness   conceptual sandblast
on a stubborn issue
what a difference a pronoun makes
in waking nice and easy
a place to savor

10

easiest Sunday pleasing
trips the accusative clause
and disjunctive grace shines stupidly
you're a brazen life
what a Mexico
sexy rain sounding
more like a turn for the better
I, you and everything
once again fucking speech
to lie in seriously individual slumber
wake up and be still!
feel that different engine turning
book with memory
but stick around for this

11

what's standard blows the lily
what a mother
recognize me teeming in slow butter
release is a thing worth craving
everything waits at the bistrot baby
just like me
step on it in a soft mint bed
in a tall cherry glove
hey, what a mind
dip me in mashed potatoes
and flip the brazen waltz on
engineer the turn off C onto E. 7th
then speak green to me
spliced is always right

12

so you left, you bastard, so what?
I'm ready to include the world
through with internal wars
weather's clear
and lies are angels in the snow
best be off and running babe
one messy satellite still hovers
you are the one and only blinking muscle
God's a shiny fuck
step on your own toes to keep someone
else from beating you to it
the bathtub isn't long enough for four
don't dream now   float
it's the best with Sunday morning peaches

13

snow drips in the airshaft
what castlelike bricks inside and out
the best is heat waking up the pipes
or blue green sea bubbles
in a morning tub
books still boxed under one bed
as tiny ticking breaks through
the 6 a.m. day
all night awake and stubbornly happy
there's a sink of words to tend to
everything slept to Chopin
and the lips kept moving and imagining
a concept of a life in hard surfaces
or a bend of rest in eyes or thought

14

gray light on gray walls
tells the time or else the rain
or snow or wet worry
has saturated the sky
now a wave of green blue
no–gray blue turning planets
time for a peanut butter sandwich
and Lapsang Souchong tea to sandblast
the brain cells and give an active
push to memory and pronouns
busy self to lose self
to find self losing self in busyness
ouch! a stressful one
will stay and play away the gray

15

silly windows–too many in one messy room
to liberate a beating wing of change
let's start with a green breath
then still in the red comfort
wait or rather run–no–recognize
what planet–what life exists
so don't believe lies
saturated with busy slumber
drums are beating at Gargoyle Mechanique
above–the stage is set for April with Artaud
and stubborn grace rides me
through the rhythm energized
by my own knotted talk and dreams of change

16

meeting at the Ukrainian National Home
talk is short–jaws tight
you appear by chance
as if to remind me that change is pain
silly chatter floats on the surface
we can't look at each other
eyes shutting out memory
smiling tightly a cough
signals difficulty–resistance to change
kitchen closing–scent of ammonia hovers
once comfort meant pursuit
now comfort means avoidance
you catapult toward the door
pushed by half a table of disapproving eyes

17

what an individual concept
poets waxing suicidal
as spring comes in a blue storm
your vast shiny mind
hovers in a taxicab
on Broadway below Canal
she stubbornly insists
on remembering friendship
making the connections between thought
and muscle–between muscles and mind
between belief and a single bed
we mess around with the beat
of resistant chatter
finding a difficult pleasing best

18

the car moves slowly in a rainstorm, tears also
news flash comes after sticky worry, there are no villains
this is a serious concept bright and spinning between avenues C & D
1:25 a.m. brain cells busy messing around with stubborn friendship
he says he thought about me in Montauk
I was afraid to ask exactly what he thought
remembering his thinking of me
while rocking the boat with someone else in Amsterdam
it's summer and we cannot do what we cannot do
painful resisting gray boundaries and limitations
an individual proclaims: we are not villains
I blamed you & I blamed you & I blamed you also
but please forgive my lack of generosity
my thoughts are too Byzantine to please you

19

I forgot you with Donnatol & too much wine on the Upper West Side
a midget runs through the party as I admire the grapes on Amber's hips
who are we to sleep through ecstasy?
you are fairly happy you say–will be away all summer
I don't blame you, still what has changed?
I cry in the morning & in the evening before sleeping
I follow an uneasy downward moving through my day
still smiling seems a formal connection
if heard in a voice on the phone or imagined before sending a postcard
and so our long introduction continues
I shy away from groups as you cultivate them
a crazy burning keeps us faithful to a memory
of peaceful blue beds & pure light
we'll meet there soon to drown all thoughts of loss

Middle

1

I have no words
they have me again
speechless but spilling over
thought

I don't understand
actions repeat themselves
the man walks out the door
but this time the raincoat is black

a light comes on
brighter than before
but less is seen
a small room
or a small portion
of a room

he says "I can't remember
now – where am I?"
he asks for help
someone answers "page 15,
we're on page 15"

the chocolate cake looks
tempting with raspberries on top
but it's not real
made of Styrofoam

the lights dim
then a close-up
the inside of a pocket
red

a knock at the door
no one answers

this is my message
there's a key underwater
moving–
the surface of the water–
not the key

it's 1:27 a.m.
quiet
words won't leave me

2
to be alone with it
to watch it moving
this isn't a trick
the hand shakes too much
to reach

1:32 a.m.
I have none
certain new phrases distilled
woke up thinking "I want"
dare not

4 a.m.
sped through Sappho
& *Lying Together*–a novel

for quite some time
dark ceiling counting space

for some reason
the last straw fell on my back
Queen Tyi, wife of Amenophis III
18th Dynasty Cairo grimaces

carezza–
                the woman is bleeding
                she keeps
                his cock inside her
                till they sleep

have to think of structure
narrative
too long in the middle
then the end
why not begin
with the middle

standing still
is no answer
nothing ever
stands still

movement as in
particles shifting
also 2 particles
existing in the same space

3
A voice–
"never seen you
with so little
clothes on before"

it's 5 a.m.

Suddenly Everything

Funky Sonnet #1

a purpose sometimes resembles a cow
in an alien pasture enough said
and bred to fill all the circle stores
in all the malls in america
filled with circles and cows
and a little remembrance
clothes falling in a meadow
resumes patiently continuing
yes in an approximation of a dream
but then dreams are too easy we
must remember action and easy
access to circular gardens
and perpendicular progress
among the tules at noon

Funky Sonnet #2

but then how is it not a ladylike
gesture to straddle a friendly poet
in my jean skirt on a weeknight
or was it a lazy afternoon well
whenever it was it was dear and
much like a lady as in a woman
as in honest desire or a bit
of holy communion or holy communing
do you never wear socks
i'm not looking out the window
i'm looking ecstatic or some
understandable facsimile
freewheeling in my own psychic space
i'm often fond of freefalling ladyfingers

Funky Sonnet #3

in my movie i'd shoot a woman
walking through her day
careful attention to dress hems
and footsteps–fingertips–
soupspoons–eyelashes–doorknobs–
backs–umbrellas moving
beneath i'd hear a voice describing
random scenes from dreams and
fragments of conversations
also much street sound and
occasionally the breath
slo-mo frames of the fluctuating
expressions of her face

Galloping Personas

so the mask remains baffling
say hello to the mask
a new way of being a "Person"
or a hurricane Cordelia in Biloxi beauty
there's a mountain out my window
and you must wear a golden blouse

reading this a golden blouse
may seem somehow baffling
out the American airplane window
is an unidentified flying woman mask
of quilt-like patterned asymmetrical beauty
i'm packing–it's raining–i'm a person

retelling the personal
story–walking for our mothers in a blouse
of golden–sleeping–whispering beauty
her name was Jackie Gleason, baffling
just listen to your heart and the mask
the pre-focus flies out the window

what's hip? who knows? who cares? not the window
i remind them of a galloping person
dreaming again–let the mask
go–let us know when you find it–the blouse?
"the key's on the Hawaiian nude" baffling
did you kiss my back and murmur another beauty's

name–just for fun–let's investigate beauty
the historic, poetic window
of this event is ever baffling
H.D. was called "Dactyl" "Hildy" "Person"
Bryher was always "He" in a blouse
but really "Winifred" in her "fido" mask

she wants to go into analysis in Brazil–masking
nice dogs have no teeth but rare beauty
he said "wow" "oh" said she in her golden blouse
fill up the sound window
the play's the carriage and a person
sings of the secret boarder, baffling

songs of a baffling secret mask
experiencing persons of great beauty
by love's window in a golden blouse

I oughta get the atomic bomb out of the car
Now in a limited Hollywood engagement
I gotta go to the hospital to see one of my members
                    The Black Drama
2 thumbs up for Mother Teresa
I bet they hated *Blue Velvet*
Suddenly everything is different
Every weekday morning
                              The issues are real
Sudden Death
            A Manager of McDonald's
in the armpit of the Cesspool in the Bronx
                    Guardian Demons
When they see something the group leader
signals the street patroller
Just noticing how you fit in the world
On a one-way trip to Palukaville
Pop had to become a star out of sheer necessity
Conversation always seems to tire me
Eddie Foy in pink satin
I don't wanna see it
Let's go back to the candy store
Don't fool around with a star
                        More licorice
Thanks father I can just make the second act
Is it not true, however, that the pressures
that will be brought jamming the streets
Active length for active hands
We kids figured he was planning a mass murder
I bet you it's something good for us
It's out of this world
Everybody's become a critic
Oops there goes another one
We can't afford to lose an American congressman
What happened to that sweet little boy you used to be
Get your feet out of the fish tank Michael
You may have heard
At Merrill Lynch we believe your investment options
know no boundaries
Cool Whip

Hours

This is an angry poem

I am not a primordial princess
I am not a jazz expert
I am not an exotic adventure
I am not a great tap dancer
I am not an outstanding athlete
I am not a criminal
I am not a sex fiend
I am not the other woman
I am not an inappropriate choice
I am not an embarrassment
I am not a trophy for the radically chic
I am not a radical politico
I am not a crusader
I am not a revolutionary
I am not a southern accent
I am not a nice white boy's fantasy
I am not a rapper
I am not fluent in "Black English"
I am not a symbol of integration
I am not a token anything
I am not your black friend
I am not your black girlfriend
I am not an expert on Harlem
I am not more white than black
I am not assimilated
I am not your secretary
I am not your gateway to Africa
I am not the voice of Black America
I am not the other
I am not a threat
I am not a typical anything
I am not the "Black Experience"
I am not to be pitied
I am not to be praised unnecessarily
I am not a decoration
I am not the keeper of ancient wisdom
I am not a part of your mythology
I am one black woman

10 Hours on a Sunday

a long beautiful walk
great idea but whose

mild aching reminds me
of a body–a life

a lovely walk
with little left

time to buy
dark glasses

midway down
and the sound turns

time for fried chicken
or spaghetti or sleep

yes time for chicken
spaghetti doesn't do it

sitting satiated
and almost painless

what a pretty song
kids playing outside my window

and the payoff
is a kind of power

shapeshifter
(inspired by the introduction to Anne Waldman's *IOVIS*)

boy/child/trickster
he is one
   he is two
he is three
      innocence/genuine/pure spirit
& mischievous
wild child/jester
he can be many

hold me–enfold me
   wrapping–the word wrapping
comes to mind as in
enraptured
   wrap me in this complex rapture
the moment when
 we are caught up
  drawn up
    taken up
        to split the sky
  divide the heavens
he is shifting forms
clouds/trees
   soft furry creatures
smooth cold stone
relief
transmigration/transmutation
transformation/transfiguration–
a trance in any thing

I look at you
& see my mother's eyes
compassion
caretaker/nurturer/facilitator
compelled to soften rough travel

I look at you
& see my small self
screaming

Love and Landlords

the pentecostal church sits
with the shadow of a cross
and blue and yellow
stained glass windows
my thoughts cut up
like my mother's hands
in that dream
she came to visit
i led her away from knives

our ideas of sharing and co-existing seem out of balance–out of synch one from another–she says "I wouldn't mind if we shared him" like Laura biting my triple chocolate cake–my mud pie in Yaffa's with ever adorable Virginia who's always "action-packed" and there too once J.D. someone I once loved not being in love with him while he was with another not in love with her but she was with him and I was his other–his woman in the city and this after breaking up with Jo Jo who once loved J.D. not of course being in love with him which Rennie said was the crucial difference–somehow still grieving for the loss of Jo Jo who I ever sing the blues for in many variations I felt closer to J.D. who had also loved him once and perhaps still does but J.D. said over pizza that he saw a therapist because of his inability to maintain a long term relationship after his break-up with Kathleen who Jo Jo promptly comforted and she found another Jeffrey soon after in Santa Cruz

they put up a petition
in my building
to build a playground
in the present
garbage dump
across the street
instead of housing
i suppose because
it touched a school
they put a fence around
evacuated the garbage
flattened out the clay
now red mud piles against
the new gray fence
after: rain, sleet, snow

no history is final

                                         what is it to love

     the way your hands feel

                                                my back against a carpet

                 your eyes slow

                             and serious

      low sounds moving

                       like the room's breathing

          what is it?

something to do with generosity of heart and mind and body and the
familiar sound of a voice–the vibrations of a voice moving through
your body

First Hour

men and women
men and women
a separate language between us
understood only in the clinches
loving men in a diner on East 16th
in an office on 20th and B'way
in an apartment–Crown Heights, Brooklyn
in Williamsburg, Brooklyn
in San Francisco's Upper Haight
on Berkeley's Telegraph Avenue
loving women strolling across Union Square
squeezing zucchini

there once was a name for this
long ago
perhaps not in English
a word meaning: I love you although I don't understand you
meaning: please decode my message
meaning: something to do with my flexible arch
               as it touches the sole of my shoe
meaning: perhaps tomorrow there will be a difference

Brewer's Yeast stinks like piss
it's supposed to be good for you

I'm creating a healing crisis
meaning: it has to hurt to feel better
meaning: pleasure=pain in some translations
she said "I'd really like it if you weren't always drunk
               when we make love"
he misunderstands: "You mean you want to see other people?"

loving men and women in conflict
loving men and women in constant change

I love the freckles below your left shoulder blade
        I bless this space with love

in an acceptable time
this would be acceptable
but as you're rolling on the carpet
as you're banging against the wall
you're nodding out on a bus window
you're shooting up in "the Projects"
you're not touching me
in order to be seen
not touching me
saying no meaning yes
saying maybe meaning no
considering this moment
I must reconsider

Second Hour

if I were the Savior
you would lose again

"we went to all the gay clubs and had a very wild time"
she said sipping blood in a wine glass. what seemed stranger
still was a tale of a quadriplegic's bride (bought for the
weekend) and the way his voice was amplified so that
words closely resembled loud echoic (loudly resonating)
moans

if I were a sailor
you would loose again

"there doesn't seem to be a balance of interest in our conversations"
there's a balancing machine that measures exactly the flow of air
emitted from each vent in a given room or cluster of rooms

if I were a saver
you would lease again

"I feel used" she said. "As if a relationship is an economic
arrangement," he said

I now release the need to be a victim
I now release the need

if I were a saint
you would leave again

I ask "What have I done?"
"Nothing...the little things add up"

my thoughts point vindictive daggers in your direction

are we having fun yet?

                be my friend
                        be my overcoat
                                be my remote control
                                        be my barometer
                                                baby

Third Hour

I'm just moaning on my own
in a subdued and goodly crimson
black bottomed out
with rockabilly blues

      where am I now?
this is certainly an unfamiliar place
I've spent too much money again

"I want him but I'm not obsessed with him.
This is new for me" she said,
"this is frightening"

if I were a man what would I like
to think like?

she continues to talk
      her mouth moving swiftly
      glasses above her nose
      moving slightly
      she lifts her skirt
      below the table
      she scratches her left thigh
      exposing a stockinged leg
      to the rest of the diner
      she readjusts a few things
      and returns the skirt
      to its former resting place
      hem lightly hitting
      below the knee
      she continues talking

I see a back of a head
      or a body
that must be him
      but couldn't be
I hold my breath
      and blink
several times quickly
      before continuing

I'm not doing this very well
      so wanted it to be finely crafted

Fourth Hour

"what do you have to do to be an artist?"

        with flat shoes
        wear black words
        to Bliss Deli

     go for more radical collage
     and a permanent place
     with the Portable Dante

when discovered it was a small blue blaze

        she was late
        for a meeting
        with her therapist
        found Linda Evans
        in her bathroom
        ripping her shower curtain
        and she kept trying
        to piece it back together
        but Linda kept ripping it
        into neat little squares

the fire burned quite successfully for several days
turning the sky above the fields a thick gray
no one tried to stop its progress no one knew how

Fifth Hour

you know me by my word

such a lovely arrangement
of people waiting
on the subway platform
such a beautiful design
a choreography of fidgets
and weight shifting
        each person has a different focus
eyes zeroed in on a speck of asphalt
a rat in the tunnel
a poster for a new Richard Gere film
down the tunnel searching for a light
that says: train's coming

"he didn't expect me to walk out–
he expected me to beg him..."
her hands opening and closing
over half a cantaloupe
"you know" he said
"I should have stayed longer–
I would have had more time with you"

jacketed in another's life
I feel at home, cozy
reluctant to slip out again
into my own

it's raining today
they say snow soon
I need boots
I love those black barked trees
bare and soaking wet
branches like lace
against Chelsea lofts
        my hour's over

Sixth Hour

I wanna go to Barcelona
I wanna go to Amsterdam
back to San Francisco
but here–this city
what a poem
what is a poem?
            beauty in language
                a woman hesitating over yams
                at Farmer's Market

                              a man baseball cap intact
                              hawking umbrellas
                              on East 16th & B'way

We now serve delicious
Espresso Coffee $1.00
at Jason's Restaurant & Cocktail Lounge

        Old Fashioned Mint Julep
    Manhattan Bloody Mary
                Alexander Martini
      Imported Heineken on Tap

I wanna go to London
I wanna go to Paris
I wanna go to Uruguay
I wanna go to Istanbul
Tokyo, Budapest, Munich, Vienna, Mexico
            I wanna go

Seventh Hour

She says "Poems are easy once you know how to make them"
and I'm tempted to believe her.

He is from Spain–he confuses the verb "to do" with "to make"
Everyday I attempt to do a poem–to make a poem sing.

She doesn't seem that tall or that pretty and he doesn't even
introduce me–I introduce myself–why shouldn't I?

Spain or San Francisco? I need flowers today and a lover–
quickly or rather several separately and then simultaneously.

Today is a day I need to be famous–I need excessive attention–
the focus of a million eyes on my fingertips and eyelashes.

Slept 13 hours last night and still feel a vague fatigue
and toothache–Dr. Janof's Christmas gift.

I think all women should be adored for the simple miracle of
their existence.

Mom said "You're a special person to me and to God–don't you
ever forget that" and I cried a bit behind my desk and typewriter and huge
brown console phone and my stack of papers and messages and packages
because I believe for a while I had forgotten.

Yes flowers and perhaps good friends today instead of lovers
and also a good poem or two–yes!

He said "This was written to an old lover of mine who's here tonight
and she knows who she is" I wondered if she did.

She said "His work is an interesting combination of some things
very old and also very new."

How can I separate emotions and my body from the words I use?
Why must I?

So much to do, none of it important–except maybe eating and
sleeping and watching the sunset.

There was something else I wanted to tell you but I've forgotten
what it was.

Eighth Hour

Don't know exactly what I expect from the world
        other people
        myself
All I know is
        something more
        happiness or beauty
All I know of love are the fairytales
        and brief moments of intense connection
        being transported by beautiful words on paper
        by beautiful arms around me
        by beautiful thoughts surrounding me
And so many memories
        hard to sort them out
        the real and the imaginary
My body is weak and lifeless
        I'm living on pure spirit and will
There's only enough left of me to be hurt yet again
        holiday sadness comes with a palm reader:

"The color of your aura is lavender but you are very sad and so it's gone down to deep purple, your lucky number is two, a tall, dark, handsome man loves you– you will have two children–a boy and a girl and settle in a place where it's warm all the time, in two weeks you will get a phone call that will make you very happy, in two months you will make a trip, there is a woman friend of yours with light hair who is very jealous of you–watch out for her, you were born for good things, you are very sensitive, creative, you will find what you want–there will be a change in your job. I need to meditate to bring your aura up–for three days I will go to my church and light candles and meditate for you and you will feel like a burden has been lifted."

She wore heavy black eyeliner
curling toward the edges of her eyes

Ninth Hour

so so gray
and a graininess of vision
slow motion movement
a tall man in a long black cape
turns quickly to face me
cape twirling wide in the wind
I am not allowed to see his face
only a blinding light
in the place
where his face would be
my view of him
from a very low angle
looking into the light
of his face
I must be kneeling
or lying on my belly
on a cold
cement surface
there are walls surrounding
a courtyard
gray also and very high
I see the tops of dark lifeless trees
and sky above the walls
there is also a voice

Tenth Hour

a variation of the truth
overheard a man upstairs;
"So many times I wanted to say I love you"
body moving very slowly
mind too quickly
a creaking floorboard

"the receiver was on my prunes"
says the revolutionary thinker
and inventor of the geodesic dome

"ambiguous talk about the thing"
before falling into a well

Savoy Corner Pizza
Disco Donut Coffee Shop
Arabella's Reception Area
in many ways
we are one in the same
thing

on newsprint:
black with white lettering
cover of sturdier material

14 stations of the cross
stages of the Passion
"Why did you forsake me?"

what resembles the world?
how do you put a label on that?
where does it fit?

walk of Via Dolorosa
"The bottom is geometric Matisse
and the top–
                    then the dahlias..."

Twelfth Hour

he says he had his first aesthetic experience
at the Hirshhorn in front of I forget which
painting–he says it fondly like a devout
Christian's "I was saved on June 5th
1953 and I've been a soldier for our Lord
ever since."

should devotion be a requirement for friends
or lovers?

requirements for lovers:

1. a bit stubborn and difficult
   but only enough to keep things exciting
2. should not adore foods that make me
   nauseous
3. no compulsive nail biting, toe tapping,
   finger snapping, knuckle cracking or
   nervous twitches
4. a highly developed sense of the absurd
5. mildly depressive or anxiety prone
   with optimistic tendencies
6. limited fanaticism
   and
7. assorted adorable traits

Zither Mood

for Bernadette

trembling little female bear
burning pigeon-toed little girl bear
paws cupped–an inverted prayer
a casual mudra held at the crotch

i always stand watching door closing
kiss my forehead–my cheek
see my hand brushing your hair from your face
stroking hair fur fuzzy halo

such a pretty little bear big girl man woman
such a pretty one with such violent thoughts

such a pretty momma bear poppa's going
such a way with words and women
such a way with big bear hugs
beer brewing up blood and sex
fire red faced bear in constant agitation
i hold your hand for strength

Little Nothings

oh what today
what today what
spinning away in air
and spying crystal facets
of the world in fragments
wide eyes on subway platform
dreamy intoxicated walk at party
trembling fingers grasping cigarette
a face   a whole world
waiting to envelop
what seems to be   me
at such a particular time
such timely particulars
          spin

carrying an expression of noble suffering
can be exhausting (not like a movie)
he loved my sad eyes
"seen in the living they are doing"
a long time ago after breakfast
"you ask me, I ask you. This is love"
"we must be more intellectually wild!"
whales are singing while we're sleeping

attachment: desiring to hold
                    forever
the elegance of joy co-existing with suffering
the ideal: face smiling with a single tear
                    falling
"you must suffer for love"
          says Israel watching
(one who wrestled with the angel)
                    clinging–grasping

powers of names–hyphens rising
I am so fickle in my world view
what the world knowing would

speeding through my body
sitting in the Radiance Room
               I am dead
               I am dead
I am dead today and always
eyes that never see
ears that never hear
mouth that only whispers
into certain ears

yes, she's hungry
running a competitive race
and making stakes on indecision
devours whole afternoons
a flake   a sun   a poodle
fragile bird
keeps pace with wind
hiding broken bones
whole centuries disappear
behind eyes
appetite growing into invisibility
she tastes the subtle body
not enough wanting
not enough sleep

Untitled

language is essentially
the same
under differences
people are essentially
ambiguous
my hands and feet
are always colder
than the rest
of my body
his hair
all over his body
is very long
and fine
and energy
is always
separate ends
of the same
thing
her pale toes
were black
with mud
that night
and i saw
the lawn sprinklers
on broadway
water pedestrians
also
if they
jaywalked.

Zither Mood

1

you said "sometimes lap dancers wear pearls"
you said you'd "give me pearls"
found I was laughing in my sleep last night
don't know what was moving through my sleep
I crave popcorn
"popcorn love" just like the boys
in Miranda Sex Garden
who look so much like girls
what was I thinking
only noticing the flood light through the window
and a wild fuzziness of sensation
perceptions juggling together
like the two vodka tonics and the sips
of McSorley's dark in my tummy
I call up these emotions and they set
my neurotransmitters popping
in stereo–no polyrhythmic layering jamming
the system–lower back aching
my boyfriend says from too much Pepsi
affecting my kidneys
why don't I find the Yugoslavian journalist
attractive–why ask why
when a sliver moon smiles down

2

first thing this morning
almost waking–thought
"the sliver moon looked down on us"
then the phone rang
a woman with a chipper voice
asked for the number of the former tenant
I gave it to her my voice rasping and scratching
and even 15 minutes after I found my glasses
my eyes wouldn't focus
I wonder if you'll call
I should clean up my back room
and start reading the encyclopedic
tome *This Business of Music*
on which I spent my last dollar
buying last night
and trudged through the first
snow of the season to find
this is a poem of dailiness
or is this a poem of dallying
this is one of my first days off
when I have absolutely no
commitments–long time since
I've felt this kind of lazy freedom
this is a journal like poem
a rattling off of minutia with
things of great import hiding
in the corners–I love
what hides in the secret
corners of poems like codes
begging to be broken
have to wake up (stop) my tea is cold

session

pop filter
dense Doughty
I already did caffeine
e.q.
fly-in sound
super bottom
what if I said I could
change all that
just playing changes
walking behind the beat
electric bass just
doesn't swing
detritus
the circle on your boat
torture time album
he's a monster
where objects will fall
giant steps
real sledgy
dance hall dirgy
don't want to
site you any signals
Haitian drumming
is some sick stuff
if things crash
music will become reality
it's still thrilling
to hear great slapping
I was pretty out then...
more out
it was funky
but more out
the origins
of drama
and the future
of fun
through a cloudy
medicine mirror
time
well it's
not exactly an
objective thing

Rose Window (or Prosettes)

ROSE WINDOW (or Prosettes)

Queer nuzzling into a new day. Daisy woke up. Fear woke her up–a new ghost to go dancing with. Several hours later. Miss the world and its resonators, bald heads walking, laughing babies, men with canes, creeping ivy and grapevines. Gentle sleeve-tugs. It is a thing that happens. Before crossing a street he kissed her. She saw his eyes zero in on her lips and his torso bent forward. Her eyes locked on his lips and as she aimed hers slightly to the left they landed cheekward somewhere hovering between his beard and the air. Their chins touched briefly as she imagined his arms around her, hands on her ass and his tongue deep in her mouth. The light changed. A small drizzle. Fear woke Daisy up in the middle of the street.

After having his cock in my mouth two-times-over the night before, I went to the P.O. to pick up what turned out to be the present I'd sent him for his birthday. It had been sent back to me labeled: Dead Mail Matter. Walked out of the P.O. into the snow thinking how he felt inside me–when it went on and on and he didn't come but I did over and over.

Breakfast at Veselka's: I ate everything on my plate quickly without feeling I was eating at all, my real body somewhere else. And the sun blasted through the window behind him so that I couldn't really see his face–the details of his face elsewhere with my body–my mouth. Eating then seemed not as real as it had been in my dream the night before. Although in the dream I only looked at food I saw spread out on rows and rows of tables. But somehow looking became eating.

Stood up in the ancient four legged tub, water falling from me, took the large pink towel from his hand and quickly dried myself as he stood beside the tub, eye fastened on the telly. Then he raised his hand and placed it in space–settling as if on an imaginary armrest in the manner of an Elizabethan gentleman. I glanced at the hand baffled somehow, searching briefly for meaning then climbed out of the tub without assistance, on my own power.

"Since it is more difficult to think in terms of simultaneity than in terms of sequence, we begin to conceptualize the movement in terms of adirectional trajectory." Jessica Benjamin from *The Bonds of Love: Psychoanalysis, Feminism, and the Problem of Domination*

Everyone suddenly blue, a dark effervescent blue as if covered with body paint–

dressed for carnival. But somehow it was caused by a shift in the lighting–

suddenly everyone resembled barking blue dogs. We began describing ourselves

to each other. He said I was all blue except for a spot of red at the center of my

lips–a deep red spot as deep as the blue that covered the rest of my body.

I felt cold. His hands touched me, his body pressed against me and I felt a vague sensation of pressure at different points on my body as if I were being caressed through layers and layers of wool. He was a slight breeze sending faint ripples across the surface of a lake. I could hear him breathing.

It was a green–sunny spring day. We stood on the sidewalk. I began to gag. Red, black blood spewed from my mouth onto the asphalt. I crouched as he knelt beside me trying to stop the bleeding by pressing his shirttails over my mouth.

Perhaps this is preparation–this slipping in and out of madness?

The day is cold and beautiful. Snow falls on Brooklyn. Though I hated the sight of the first flakes, now I'm glad.

"They do not appear, as a rule, to be integral components of our conscious psychic life, but seem rather to be extraneous, apparently accidental occurrences." Jung

He said his fantasies are usually more abstract. He hardly ever focused on a specific person or as in this case on merely the hands of a specific person.

I see rocks, twigs, old bricks, dry weeds. All moving below me. No, I must be moving. In a moving vehicle. Perhaps a train. Looking out of a window to the ground below.

I was hungry. So I decided to clean out the refrigerator. Ran into the living room and turned up the TV so I could hear it in the kitchen as I cleaned. Left the glass top of the vegetable "crisper" in the sink with the water running.

I got back and started scrubbing the top of the crisper. I was thinking, he said the night before that he was leaving soon for Hanoi, then the glass shattered. The floor, the countertop, the sink—full of shards of glass.

"You're so beautiful" he said. He was stroking my back, the long slope of my back. Somewhere there was a tape recorder playing. I heard the sound of my own voice reading a text I'd written. When my voice stopped, his continued. I was in a bright pink motel.

what is a true thing

how true can a thing be

one thing–how can it be true

when all else is added

is it more true

more truth

the statement and

its antithesis

We were lying in bed pulling the dark brown comforter around us. There was a knocking sound. But no one was at the door. We tried to sleep and speak quietly of those things you only speak of in bed–but the knocking, banging sound kept distracting us–as if someone were trying desperately to get in or out.

She kept dropping things, her appointment book, her script, a peach, and fidgeting, finding new things to eat. Her dark tan standing out against white shorts and T-shirt, rustling papers and paying little attention to the progress of the class. Later while she was on stage working on a monologue from Bergman's "Fanny and Alexander" she explained that she was always amazed by and at the same time afraid of the wonderful lush world that seemed to open up in her mind while on stage–as if she wasn't good enough–couldn't be worthy of such imaginative splendor. So on stage she kept moving and breaking her concentration and off stage she dropped things.

I sat by the window of my favorite cafe watching a woman seated at one of the tables outside. Adoring the way she slouched and the mixture of sadness and boredom in her eyes, I pointed her out to the gentleman sitting across from me. He said, "A fine example of Yuppie discontent. I wouldn't want to be her boyfriend." I ignored his comment except to wonder why he couldn't see the beauty I saw: her reddish hair, blunt cut, dressed all in gray, a single empty glass on the table in front of her. I loved the way she gazed into the distance as a way of saying: "There is no salvation anywhere but why should I give up searching?"

She had burning red hair and her nearly translucent skin stretched tightly about the bone–pale blue eyes staring from the skull–a ghost kept in motion by desire. She was in love with an Irish folk singer she'd never met.

He said, "that train was slow as shit!" and I wondered about the truth of that expression. After all doesn't it all depend on the efficiency of your digestive system?

Reminds me of this woman who really took the expression "You are what you eat" to extremes. She claimed that you are what you expel. In other words: you are your shit, she even wrote a play about it. The main character was a Ladies Room attendant in a sleazy downtown dance club who also had an extreme and extensive scatological philosophy. This was the woman one ex-love-of-my-life took up with after we broke up. Amazing.

As his girlfriend tried to be friendly and asked me to hire her, I stood shifting my weight from one foot to the other, occasionally looking into her eyes trying to determine whether she had anything particularly beautiful about her. She mentioned she was performing soon at the Lizard's Tail in Williamsburg and I thought of the night her boyfriend thrust his fingers up my cunt and the sound of his breathing as he stroked his cock and I held his balls as he came.

I remember yelling and screaming–holding onto an open car door as it pulled away dragging me through the street.

Radical Doubt

Radical Doubt

this is strange–what is strange–opening up a place–inventing sound to fill space–to begin again then again to say or echo a voice–a thought–mind slips–this odd configuration living this–several patterns submerged and then rising again–tight chest–too many faces–terrible time–fill in the C-spot–stand still–stop–I will stop here–this is time to stop–is disengagement the prelude to total implosion?–saturation point–scale the world down to where it fits

my dreams are missing for several days–almost a week, maybe over a week–time shrinking and expanding–a flexible tunnel. want my dreams back

odd that all can be resolved by talk–the act of speech–uttered in the right ear equals release

why do you ask "in an ideal world what would you want?" when worlds–the many are never ideal–philosophizing again, becoming too metaphysical–you will never be willing to make my ideal world happen

she says: does it, did it, did she, he, it move, touch you? well did she? would you tell me–loving minds and breasts–did it move–the earth–the mind–the lace curtains–did they? does it touch you–me–she at all–being an introvert only my perception of his touch touches me and being an extrovert you adjust to the object–objectively rearranging matter–logistically planning placement of wrists, ankles

"I could never make love to a woman if I didn't like her ankles" he said. I've never noticed ankles before as being particularly attractive or repulsive–similar motivations–intensity

screamed as you watched my hand mutating in the dark and she appeared to rise from the grave or slither from the ground to her full height in the sudden shaft of light–a doorway–opening

a portly man underwater rock climbing writes a poem about us–never seen so many people naked she said not since high school–the flaky one builds a sand castle on the rocks–you say she unnerves me because of my fear that I may be like her–she opens a door–strikes a nerve–a familiar pattern I detest

evil–yes–idea of a demon in the room a dark presence just like before–pre-utterance–crying in your sleep–sobbing in your sleep this time–spiders fill the house–I woke up happy this morning she paced back and forth in the canyons–detached–finding inner roads more comfortable–stuck dancing in place–your face glows from sun–a burnished rose and also joyous–watching the dyad turn I marvel at the binary system expanding to allow further entry then closing in again–folding inward or rearranging into another similar pattern always opening again–a lust for openness–a need for the entrance visible

Variations on the Blues for Jo Jo #10

try if language is desiring in a different machine, then poetry is the
typewriter chimeras, the here I am at the temporary poet in particular has
at my supreme essence or ideal desk before the images model of that
machine my lover never been able to find I want to see himself or herself
again, and feeling all our desires are rejected again once in our
languages written, eyes so bright today remains helplessly lips so full
my mired position of thee my photo sung, painted, played, that slight off
otherwise signed or signaled, my other disintegration left centeredness
from defunct generations. and in music, painting, makes me

Variations on the Blues for Jo Jo #11

Jo continues to maintain the art of skull-
ture–still falling bronze dreams in the sand owls
pregnant cats randy monkeys. angel, this monument,
this mosaic, this gravestone with quilted
collage–we–the height of our–yes–with the simple
paint, canvas, bronze language, our brutality, our
madness, our understanding. i need "black holes" yet
we pro-seed with so rejected so ideally secret
meanings clearly, obviously contemporary
signings, truly poetic primal desirings functioning
as such in his face as one. the truth is, poetry,
membered mentality–elements of ink iron sound.
every individual is of course in the darkwood of the
idea–beyond alienation from society i've felt like
my eyes betrayed me. the piss of our insanity.
our pose of the day is to picture mess and origin of
consciousness.

Variations on the Blues for Jo Jo #13
(No it's never happened before)

you have an active mind
       and a clever fur
you will hear money
          there is yet time enough for a different path
  type another sad life
          time enough for slight lies
  voices friendly to you
  streets deeply attached to family honored
         (whispered some excuse)
  motivation craziness

        The Chinese say:
        COMFORTER CURSE–
  wandering likeness erupts silence
when touching someone who used to be madly in love with you
         use ticklish grace
         entertain
           large
             sweetly processed
               memorial
improve merit–copy–throw flute–think air–shake spittle
         seek rabbit power for awarded social summer
         and living Methuselah-document

mirrors distrust running
         which signals unwrinkled voices
            as acting etching shifts Westbeth
                 fair seat where underground
(stretched thereabouts mood children–
        summer's grace ready)
              lived favorable rattler
              family guest

Variations on the Blues for Jo Jo #14

things opening: high/low path
        robes signal restful side
the Captain underground pressing
                complicates the problem
        neither will nor infection
                pulls saint's verdict
                or soul's separation
the voice of my beloved morning creature
        how beautiful are thy feet with shoes

at present news
        your stitched head is holding fine
results of another week's interior oblivion
        the word brought sudden fear
                a city holding nothing
                        inspires longing

I didn't know him very well but still there were intimations of abstruse
        consequences
I fell all too soon under a mirror of floating cheer
        standing here out large and beside myself with what might appear to be
the sweetest afternoon air
                time teaches to know and Sophia explains:
                        attractive things like December
                        teaches the law of palace towers
                        and the Captain's voice

still dark bark and long green lawns settle in
                        what is missing is another form of self love
other than the love of a specifically chosen other
        other than the jumbled consolidation
        of our childhood nightmares
what is needed is not a neat reflection of suffering
        not a complimentary participant in hell
what is needed so is what is so
                and what has been forgotten
        a replacing of what's been stripped away
        and a stripping away of the unnecessary
building a shield that is all embracing and welcoming
                        IF SHE BE A WALL
WE WILL BUILD UPON HER A PALACE OF SILVER
        everyone hears the warning before looking

AND IF SHE BE A DOOR
          WE WILL INCLOSE HER WITH BOARDS OF CEDAR

     silent pictures no longer recognize the world

I am a wall and my eyes are like towers
               then was I in my own eyes one that found favour.

AFTER THE MISHAP

he spent the day
drawing hummingbirds,
tomorrow elephants

"cosmic censorship"

"Phil's so cool he's
brilliant, he's in Poland...
we went to this concert
& then he became uncool...
I think he got into
the Grateful Dead"

"born from a peach"

two birds fallen from their
nest, yes, necessary—
needful in a hunt

paper beauty doll
will have been done
          this murder
soul, singular
rest before the journey
the one I admire most
among them
yes, I know, I'm watching
hands still, still
in the making
with so few words
contentment–solace
somnambulant reactions

"I'd shake all night"
"You're on my mind"
"You're worrying me"
"I've been thinking about you"
"I've been dreaming about you"

weird visitor
        multiplicity
not an organ
        but of opposites all
within the polarity
        an end

like a jewel in a toad's head
   a plea for polyandry

"take the key out
& see if the car
still runs"
"I don't care what
I think I see or dream"

must give you
gifts for the gifts
you've given me

he admired James Brown
& his polysexuality
I could kiss you all night
he said

"get comfortable &
make yourself
        homesick"

"for all of the reasons
I desired you"
"things were glowing"

yes I admit it I felt
loved–quite an accomplishment

makin' love again
with the tv on
someone talking about
wanting love or
losing love or
being in love
lots of talk
about love on tv
makes us pause

freeze frame
"got any change, young blood"

forbidden words
hide on the street
the mind must be
incandescent–free
            unimpeded

"A gift to the gods"
change for the toll

I'm a gypsy
with these earrings
& those mirrors
smiling from my breasts
my witnessing self

"are you o.k.?"
    constant checking
        for an imbalance
            a downward swing
a fall into the field of wanting
instead of your well of light
let me jump
            push me
it's so bright

now this is like a song
and you belong to...

I open the door
and the wind sings etc...
let me jump

tightness in chest
            anger
shortness of breath
            anxiety
heaviness in lower body
            depression

madness as divinity
    closer
            to the source

today he draws
        crocodiles and alligators

so it is done
it is done
in this way

baseball cap protects
him from rain
I push all of his
language buttons
  he carries me
      around
         in his pocket

I'm confounded
once again by
      possibilities

push me
I don't feel free
      to choose
I don't feel free
freedom is an alien
      to my memory

how narrow
how maddening
how stifling
can the realm
of choices be
before choice
becomes command

up against the wall
down on the floor
answer me yes or no

pull me in
it all fell down

on me
fearful
full of dread
it all fell down
a physical thing
nervousness in the body
followed by numbness
in the heart

stuck on one groove
don't know where I am

turning night's corner
"I don't want to make
you suffer"
she said

yesterday
all afternoon
he drew Amish people
tomorrow he's doing
Germany

it is becoming precious

try another number
to take me to oblivion
where could that be tonight

do you wanna smile
            from me
no–I see
how the pain
            in my eyes
excites you

how many more
  how many can I find

a story
  a belt unbuckling
    a black stockinged leg
      a glistening nipple
        an open courting carriage
two horses
    we sit tightly together

you lied to me

standing on a whale
another big fish story
story of the girl
who fell down
a deep deep hole
Messiah complex stirs
          stoops

another minor goddess
I dangle keys
in the dark

need a new myth
spontaneous meat

let's investigate
the dream machine

power plant
paralyzes heart
short-circuits the flow
of empathy

you are luminous twins
under the streetlights
of Avenue B

said you'd show me
the banana trick
          one day

telling the story
of a woman who
conceived with a drum
within the drum
a case, a box
a face, a fist
          a heart
an army of ants

let's rock
let's knock down
the doors of
heaven and horror
in the field of time

here–now
stop–wait

you lied to me

a small lie of omission
of definition of terms
big words for small sensations
or small sensations
become large visions
tell me in real time
does it get any easier
how do you remember
        beauty

Womb Dreams

Womb Dreams

Part I

mother's heartbeat
an echo of shamanic drums
ushers us into the dream
the waking trance state
where images flow
lightning energy
shooting through
        flexed muscles

     an embryo remembers
past actions
  images press beneath fluttering eyelids
and yes the drumbeat of the bearer's heart
            the bearer of the burden
                 the bearer of the gift
                    the bearer of life

she rises from bed
        it's a struggle the bearer has become accustomed to
but still her heartbeat accelerates and initiates
the unborn's trance:

            I once wore long robes
            rough scratchy wool
            brushing my ankles
            and the smell of blood
            is that here now
            or was that then?
            the smell of blood

***

all of natural history awaits us
in the mummified   fossilized excrement
  the rumblings of the ages   the sound of decay
     race to the end   and then back again

     silence is a virtue
       sweeter than the sweetest vice
         cup your hands to my breasts
            and listen
          ear to my chest
           listen to the drum
             echoing a distant shaman's beat:

he said it was an earthquake   i didn't believe him
held his hand tightly as i lay back down to sleep   he
said here comes another one   can't you feel it   can't you
feel it coming   he was blowing in my ear   i
fell asleep   woke again   he was mumbling   him
talking in his sleep   saying no   come on
come on he said i said mama no mama no   and i could feel
the blood   i don't remember screaming i don't remember it
i remember waking up frightened to   death waking up so
afraid of something   but i couldn't remember the dream
the nightmare i couldn't remember what had frightened me
but i was shaking and sweating and i thought he was i don't
know who i thought he was   i was trying to get away from
him and he kept saying it's all right it's me it's me   he
said i screamed at the top of my lungs several times over
and over and woke him up and scared him to death but i
don't remember screaming at all not hearing myself scream-
ing or feeling myself scream all i remember was being so
afraid of something   it was so dark   i didn't
know where i was or who i was
with

***

NOW there's a humming rumbling rolling sound
            a huge rock rolling   a mass of water moving
in my direction the smell of wood burning   and the sea
            somehow in the middle of the darkness   the sea
    he said: what was that?
        she: what?
        he: just before you woke me i saw a clear image of
                something–what was it?

***

                in the chapel
                on the hill
                at St. Ignatius
                i feel almost afraid to move
                the first time they frightened me
                the ornate decorations
                and yet there is such a deep stillness
                they don't frighten me anymore
                but i do feel
                in my hand is an orange tulip
                the same voices i heard
                looking up at the arches
                i still hear
                the voices of women wailing
                mourning–keening
                i try to meditate

(air is heavy here)
to pray
but what comes to me
are the voices
their presence weighing me down
and an overwhelming
feeling of
the vibrations of their weeping
a great weight but also
a calmness trapped
here for so many years
and now pressing in on me
i try to leave
their voices buried in the walls
feeling an endurance
and strength through
suffering
on my first visit
but now i can feel them
and hear them
their weeping

***

on the radio in the back seat of a taxicab
(a radio talk show)
"and now for the real stuff
and now for the meat of the matter
the blood in the pudding":

i was a man standing on a balcony
an older man–early fifties–graying hair
and people were watching from a dark court-
yard below–the balcony was half shadow

half pinkish peeling wall–a crumbling European
city–i stood there and held two guns–one at the
side of my head and one inside my mouth and fired
i don't remember pain–just a slow motion feeling
and a melting of hot liquid seeping like light
or molten rock...

***
the thoughts coming so quickly
my hands shake
a desperate tremolo
vibration of the body

can't quite remember the details

but there is something there   was something there
          so   finish it just finish   now
but something resembling a hovering round puff of solid smoke
resting at the level of my solar plexus says no not yet
       a fear catching in my gut
dear God   dear empty space   dear quiet place inside me
       send a rescuer
               send an answer to her dreams
outside the children sing: "call on Jesus, call on savior"   over and over
      like a new nursery rhyme
            "you just missed the candy man"
                       mother says.

Part II

There is no simple story, my heart isn't in it. So I'll tell it as it comes.

Something tropical–dark black earth–a rain forest perhaps. We sit on a huge boulder watching sky peeking through the trees and shadows made by the swaying leaves and branches on the ground. In the heat I feel as if we're on the bottom of the ocean and all our movements have a slow motion crispness. I feel his breath on the back of my neck–his arms wrapped around my waist. Suddenly all of the forest sounds cease–complete silence–everything has stopped. The forest becomes a soundproofed room–the air is being slowly sucked out of this beige soundproofed room making breathing difficult. He takes off his golden glasses and puts one hand on my cheek. Instantly, before his hand falls to his side I appear behind a glass window inside the room, with black velvet curtains behind me. I begin to take off my clothes. He watches. I turn my back to him and we are again on the boulder in the rain forest and I feel his hand on my bare back and his breath on the back of my neck.

Sometimes I believe darkness is purer than light. Somehow in shadows I find a fuller truth than in the blinding clarity of light. Night has always brought comfort and fear. This combination comes closer to my view of reality than one or the other existing separately.

Where is the melancholy in a chandelier, in a tenement, a stack of books on a gray wooden floor, a pair of shoes trimmed in gold? Voices always trigger the jump in the gut and then the response like bodies connected to the voices. Where inside your brain is it–this thought? Can I carve it out with a kitchen knife and save it for a better time? Can I burn it out and watch it smolder down to milk white ash and bone? I can't touch or taste or smell or hear or see it, but it finds me again and again–breath on the back of my neck.

I was running down a dark hill. It was night. They were chasing me: the men in black raincoats. I kept falling and getting up to run again just in time, before they could reach me. I reached a burnt out house and I saw someone on a top floor through a window. I went in for help but *in* was more frightening than *out*–so dark but cool and calming with many doorways charred and black with ash. Somehow I knew as I climbed the stairs again and again each time the person moved farther away, so the distance between us remained equal.

Prometheus, keen in all art, brought the fire. Little boys stomped out the flames, throwing bottles in the street, watching the pieces shatter and sparkle under streetlights.

Part III

This is the dream:

I was talking to someone–a man–about how I lit the gas and burned these things in the corner of my room–this very white room–I was also a man–I looked like David only inside I was Sarah–the man–the older man talking to me saw that I was self-destructive and as a punishment or a lesson he was going to lock me in my room and in the corner of the room was this very old sick woman dying in a huge bed–I would be locked in with her forever and I'd have to take care of her forever and the man pushed me inside and was closing the door slowly and the outside light was disappearing (sunlight) inside there was only artificial light–I was wildly throwing my hands out to stop the door closing on me and he began to push my hands inside the room so he could close the door–it was just about to close...

> "It's me–it's me"
> only a bad bright room
> and pale sun coming
> he had very heavy shoes
> somewhere I really wanted
> safety inside that room
> inside of David
> inside a man's body
> inside a woman's death
> a soft haven
> lifetime penance
> inside another's life
> keeping alive a hope of youth
> don't close the door!
> don't leave it open!
> the weapons of an old man's eyes
> what can they keep me from?

talking to someone about how she had lit the gas–burned things in the corner of her room–very white room–she was a man–she looked like David but inside she was herself: Sarah–the older man talking to her knew that she was self-destructive–as a punishment–a lesson–he was going to lock her up in her room–in the corner of the room was a very old sick woman dying in a huge bed–she would be locked in with her forever–she'd have to take care of her forever–the man pushed her inside closing the door slowly–the light outside was disappearing (sunlight) inside there was only artificial light she was wildly throwing her hands out to stop the door closing–he began to push her hands away from him–inside the room so he could close the door–it was just about to close...

> Dear David:
> How do I run in your long legs?
> tell me
> How do I not see the mountains?
> show me
> How do I not notice the sky?

                    teach me
          How do I believe I am nothing?
                    tell me
          How do I listen to my demons?
                    show me
          How do I hide from life?
                    teach me
                              Always
                              Sarah

Sarah slipped into a toughness an outward expression of David's silence–the man
was older than she was but stronger–he frightened her but her features held David's
bravado–she told him how she'd lit the match after piling the black rubber in a neat
stack in the corner of her room–watched it begin to burn–the flames excited her–
she told him this–Sarah was afraid to look away from the man's face as his fatherly
eyes became anger–hatred–he seemed to know–he knew her future–he had to stop
her–he said he was going to lock her in her room forever–she fought as the door
began to close–she could feel the old woman in the corner of the room staring at
her–she was old sick dying–Sarah was afraid–the man said she'd have to stay
forever–take care of this dying woman–but he and Sarah knew the woman would
never die–she'd be old sick dying forever and Sarah would be young and
frightened–forced to stay in that room–forced to take care of her–to nurse her back
to health–she'd never get well–Sarah would be forever nursing–the door was
closing–Sarah was crying–flailing her arms wildly to stop it–she could see a bit of
sunlight as the man pushed her hands inside and closed the door–there was no
sunlight in the room–white white walls a huge white bed in the corner supporting
the old woman–in the other corner a black scorched wall with a pile of ashes–bits
of black rubber on the floor beneath it...

          Dear Sarah:
                    How can I live with
                    your fingers inside my cock
                    your breasts crushing my heart
                    your lips pressed inside my throat
                    your eyes watching my mind
                    your toes tickling my thighs?
                    you're too large
                    for man's first birth
                    and too small to hold my fear
                              your
                              David

slipped sullen became toughness excited nurse watched white face and pile after was nothing knew the supporting closing of future then gray talking it's look going woman artificial talking sick push throwing close it's corner woman with me lesson forever old door my room had inside just was forever locked I found huge self closing crying looked care hovering light she's saying was lit someone room closing woke flames future staring flailing white black woman there begin but Sarah bits of eyes told hands staring feel though health dying she afraid forced only rubber ashes face blinding leave lock dream corner

corner crier
crooner dyer
doer dancer
prancer peering
pickled pearling
curling clue-in
denser danger
dukedom's seer
saker swimmer
smoky smiling
snakeskin sicker
soother swagger
swanker wanker
woo her whipping
whimsy whisker
woolen wagon
drank dank
downer dumpster
pressure prayer
paddle plankwood
wider westwood
winner dinner
panel player
peer some
doodle stare
some bare
fare palladium
prankster steering
bleary slackened
stone sipping
skipping spare
stand looking
leaking left
from center
right from
top stop
screeching crucial
tombstone tackle
playbill stagedoor
fire mouth
hell still

                    buckle blank
                    burr purr
                    proof fear
                    tickles

don't be afraid of who you dream you are
who you think you are
who do you think you are
so were you inside his body
did you figure largely in someone's dream
mine again
were you that old woman
were you dying
were you about to suffocate
in that bright white room
were we about to remember
something

Talks with a Stranger
(including a few words by Jorge Luis Borges)

the mirror tells me secrets
the mirror listens as I listen
the mirror speaks
            a spicy/citrus voice
tells me; my face is a Byzantine structure
      my face is a mosaic
                  a microcosm
                  a macroscope
                  a lace drawn carriage
  a light blue pool
  a light blue
      pale blue cat's eye
      pupil expanding
      an imperfect oval
                  ovulating

I said:
            hello, it was nice meeting you
the mirror said:
            nice to meet you too

I'm in the void before zero
I'm in the macaroni
I'm in the calculator
I'm in the refrigerator

F=MA Ma Mama
Force=Mass x Acceleration

Velocity=Delta D
            Change in Distance
            over
            Change in Time
            Delta T

Sun–beams of light–colored beams of light
says:

            time is a parabola
            time is cyclical
            time will tell

I was a teenage atom
a particular particle in the void
in negative time

mirror says:
    ...I know that time is always time
    and place is always and only place
    and what is actual is actual
    only for one time
    and only for one place...

the mirror shows me:
    yellow circles of light
    red and blue refracted
    tiger's webs and polar bears
    zigzag zippers–up and down

says:
    if only one could taste one's void
    if one could really rest in one's void
    and this void were not a certain kind of being
    but not quite death either

and so my life is a flight
and all is lacking
and all is forgotten
or from the other

my other–my mirror
        forgotten
    a self
        forgotten
    I say:
        hello, nice to meet you

boulder rondeau 1

all that she said
two toddlers taking turns
feet on top of the sprinkler
a literal zone of second to second swing
from friend
juice red vital and also languid
all that always there
hair tangled twisted curls back wide
sit as the lion also supplicant
language makes the thing making
smile permanent smile subtle
loving this and all restless moving
all that and always there

boulder rondeau 2

and so now what's the real story
he told her she told him he left her
then she told me that she left him
her smile like his fixed yet ambiguous
she's smiling over the spinach
he's smiling over the tomatoes
and so now what's the real thing
her headache is better now
why am I so nervous again
anxious and tight and so what's next
always holding in the tummy
the neck and shoulders the buttocks
and so what now

Gray Fox Woman

Mail Poems

in
all
her
unattractive
pointing
point taken
came or rather she had
already come
to that
the sticking or rather
thinking point
pointing politely
in front of a taxi

Hide from the little bear
      with the lover of horses
How you nuzzle my neck
      thinking of her clean shaven pussy
makes me tremble
      jump as the little mound quivers
Peace is a mind
      full of juniper trees
         & drunken bees

tall thin & all
there with 3 German Shepherds
2 poodles & a leather hat
a leather clad cat
held in her arms
protected from wind
she was fine & honest

mixing it up in
serious proportions
I stand on the edge
with flowers waiting
for his arms
to open

soft hat sways
afterglow purrs
hungry particulars
kick corners

kiss my shaved cunt
& bow to its beauty
introduce me to Dangerous
the woman in the spiderwebbed dress
the wild child filling her mouth
by the newspaper stand

let me watch you
unroll my fishnet stockings slowly
let me wait until you scream
because men *do* make noise when they fuck
but only as a form of worship

Gray Fox Woman

I want men to die of longing for me
to think of me day and night
to whine and moan like dogs
I want a kennel of moaning men
chewing anxiously at my bit
because I am so full of sun
so full of morning light
so full...
that I just wanna
fuck everybody

so what is this?
I feel so happy
so full, so free
it makes me wanna
fuck everybody

why can't I do that?
what's wrong with that?
if I can't do that
then what happens to
all this energy?

you can only dance so much
you can only sing so much
you can only write so many poems
you can only fuck the same person so much

so what do you do with all that energy
all that rolling on the grass
all that rolling on the grass
in the woods energy

I wanna fall down with rolling
on the grass women
I want gray fox women
rolling on the grass with me
I wanna ring the red bell
for gray fox women
and kennels full of moaning men

to let me know what to do
with all this energy

Poem Coming

Moving

I'm moving
can't stay inside
a thought long enough
to look around
to pin it down
but it's okay
that's the lesson
anyway
It's moving
let it go
take the flow
keep moving

one sock looks black
one looks blue from here

slipping into another's life
like a tourist
real concerns
don't concern me now
I'm living to
learn each moment
as ease & grace
I'm moving

fog covers 208
Italian lovers squirm
a thick unease
quivers around the edges
of september
bungy cord
popped on my luggage carrier

there's a white
rocking chair
in the maroon guest room
just like the one
I like to think
my mother would have
liked when she
said she'd like
a rocking chair
this one has
white cushions
with pale gray

polka dots, stripes
and frilly edges

my mother died
because she was poor

it all keeps moving

he says open up
butterfly when we make love
I look like his old love
he looks like mine
he helps me remember
the days when every
step was a mystery
now my ankles ache
I'm moving through it

he watches a stripper
as if she were a rock star
queen of glamour
he calls me love goddess
and I dance in a warehouse
at midnite after
losing my clothes

want to let it all go
but can't throw away
this yearning to know
what it is
this moment
this now
just know I'm moving

there's a fugitive puppy
camped out on the couch
and baby's brought
a stop sign home

stillness runs through
this rushing to do nothing
and I pray to know it
to hold it
hold onto it
but it's all moving
I keep moving
but it's okay

that's the lesson anyway
it's all moving
let it go
take the flow
keep moving

Untitled

eating a peach
drinking coffee black
listening to Todd
Colby on the poemfone
in between sinking
into a T.S. Eliot
essay called
"What is a Classic"
wonder if I'm
wasting my time
reading & reflecting
in a lover's apartment
in Brooklyn–
the Slope
he's gone to
decipher Shakespeare
for the day–
studying for his orals
& dropping books
off to his Italian tutor
I'm hibernating
after a night
of insomnia
reading & revolving
a stale argument
in my head
the park would
be nice
Prospect Park
the Botanic Gardens
all those roses
or back to the
subway back
to the city
clamor & clutter
I'm contemplating
a contemplative
life–or a respite
of an intense
internal spiritual
journey to come
out the other end
new & sparkling
but lethargy
sets in &
fear of finance

men are the best
distractions
while longing
to seduce
solitude as
my best and brightest
companion
I look inside
I fill my mouth

Returning

what world would I write if I were to write today?
perhaps minute details: peppermint tea leaves in the sink
or the day's sounds:

>   shrieking engines
>   sounds of the sugar plant
>   scrap metal being sifted

Charles calls to see if I'm o.k.

making notes of names of people I've met
that I'm sad I never got to know–
hey I know him
we sat around the same beer tables
he knew my face when I knew his
or I'm sure she'll remember my name
but not the body it belongs to
>   old gray heads of wisdom
I wish I'd siphoned a little off of
or great young bodies that might have
held some excitement in the holding of
>   regrets: a sign of age
or innocence?

>   to move more deeply into mystery
>   using knowledge to be innocent again
>   I'd seal the ocean into a translucent bubble
>   blown by a two year old
>   and popping on a dog's ear

1:35 a.m.–she said I don't want to see those 2 ever again–she was incensed
because we wouldn't talk about the spirituality of Bob Dylan instead of football–I
guess if we can get the zebra in and Porky the professional boyfriend Jim will
perform his primal scream into a pillow–cats on the road to food whoredom lick
the countertops–Buddha's gotten bigger by self advertising– threw up on the
Persian rug–yes I'll flush it–they really need zebras, they need silver and gold
zebras and giraffes–France is like Connecticut–that's all I need, to come home
everyday to a 4 foot gypsy woman–

>   watching forever
>   still life as fetish
>   a camera eroticizes space

smoke from the Domino Sugar Plant
sirens and buzzers from the Domino Sugar Plant
                    list #1: Sugar, Popcorn, Gingerale and butter too
                    list #2: Marlboro, Newport, Winston, Benson &
                                Hedges Gold, Salem 100's, Tootsie Rolls

taking successive time-lapsed photos
of a stolen red Buick
slowly disassembled
each night
for a month
leaving empty carcass

there's a glass dome over New York City
intensifying daymares
blood from a bald man's head
watching Puerto Rican couple embracing
pretty hooker in black on Kent Avenue
says: Good morning–have a nice Sunday

what's the matter? not much. end of subject.
next Tuesday you can vote for a Liberal

WE'LL GIVE YOU THIS GE TV
FREE!

I took my staff and swept the sky from blue to all colors of the spectrum
and I rode a multicolored magic carpet with the wind waving goodbye.

                    stained glass window bayed
                    behind his head
                    a holy meeting
                    a sermon of poets
                    head silhouetted
                    voices reverberating
                    walls holding echoes
                    we watch hands gesticulating
                    feel breath in and out
                    flies lite in hair

I woke up and then they all died

each morning consecrate yourself to be dependent
        becoming black leather knight's courtesan
returning
        many well-known and half-known faces rest here for me
I feel safe–my body secure and sure
        on the dangerous streets and trains of Brooklyn
thinking of my old knight in shining black leather
        walking in a midday downpour
leaning in Nightbreak he asks "have you ever wanted a tattoo?"

"there are slacks out there hanging like sets of venetian blinds"
        because we have language–a peculiar relationship
                separation or settling is a normal occurrence

        language is the parasite the poem invades
for a miner of huge dark plums in subway atriums
        this is perfect music for a snowstorm

how does a human being fulfill the role of
        Mother Goose in a burning palazzo
                with transposed heads

many spirits hide in the corners of our houses
        because they are not round

the baby boa's been out for two days now
        drumming heartbeats in the background
                summoning Laurie Anderson's sadomasochistic
                        narcissistic adolescent rituals

                romance is always violence
        we are ever-post-modern people

        AMERICA WAS BUILT BY TEAMWORK

says a recent TV commercial

                she looks like she's walking through a cow pasture
                she looks like she's uncomfortable in shoes
                she looks like she's always falling out of her clothes
                        they love slipping and sliding from her body
                                she's clinging–yielding–grasping

she's the softer one
she moves slowly
she loves to laugh, to giggle
      all speech beginning with a quick intake of breath
      mouth lingering over vowels
      and snapping at the consonants
      words tangled in that languid accent
she's the body

and she's the other one
the quieter one
      a small tight face
she thinks before she speaks
she moves deliberately
      always
she's well put together
she's mystery
she's the illusion
she's a deep well
she's the mind

we all have longings and desires which we try to satisfy
in this world with sensual pleasures
      if you thirst come to me
      even so I am constant in my affection for you
only a bundle of myrrh is what world I wouldn't be

Poem Coming

I feel this is the poem
stop now–must stop now
to record the poem
stop now and record
the poem–living
a familiar feeling
have I been here before?
Crosby Street is a
lovely street to walk
on an empty Tuesday
afternoon this is the poem
coming after a long time
I saw your poem browsing
through a magazine
at the Open Center on
the street called Spring
and envied your minor
celebrity and was jealous
of the love or lust
you wrote of in the poem
for someone else–
had me melancholy
turning right off
Spring to Crosby and
suddenly remembering
the voluptuous moon
the other hot June night
and another love suddenly
kissing me and
the smell of his
hair the way it
sprawled wildly
across his face
like panicked
black lace
now mingles with
the memory of the
taste of you
how you always
tasted of milk and
the buildings seem
protective now
tall and sure
on Crosby Street

and you two
nestle somewhere
in me as the poem
comes suddenly
after a long
long time

Photo: Joel Schlemowitz

Wanda Phipps is a writer/performer living in Brooklyn, NY, the author of *Wake-Up Calls: 66 Morning Poems* (Soft Skull Press), *Your Last Illusion or Break Up Sonnets* (Situations), *Rose Window or Prosettes* (Dusie Press), *Silent Pictures Recognize the World* (Dusie Press), *Lunch Poems* (Boog Literature), the Faux Press issued e-chapbook *After the Mishap* and the CD-Rom *Zither Mood*. Her poetry has been published over 100 times in a variety of publications, including the anthologies *Verses that Hurt: Pleasure and Pain From the Poemfone Poets* (St. Martin's Press) and *The Boog Reader* (Boog Lit). Her poems have also been transformed into several experimental short films by Joel Schlemowitz. She has received awards from the New York Foundation for the Arts, the Meet the Composer/International Creative Collaborations Program, *Agni*, the National Theater Translation Fund, and the New York State Council on the Arts. As a founding member of Yara Arts Group she has collaborated on numerous theatrical productions presented in Ukraine, Kyrgyzstan and Siberia, as well as in New York City at La MaMa, E.T.C. She has also curated several reading and performance series at the Poetry Project at St. Mark's Church as well as other NYC venues and written about the arts for *Time Out New York*, *Paper Magazine*, and *About.com*. For more info. check out her website: www.mindhoney.com.

Made in the USA
Charleston, SC
23 January 2010